[BOND, JAMES]

[BOND,

MICHELLE DISLER

JAMES]

alphabet, anatomy, [auto]biography

Counterpath
Denver
2012

Counterpath
Denver, Colorado
www.counterpathpress.org

Library of Congress Cataloging in Publication Data

Disler, Michelle.
   [Bond, James] : alphabet, anatomy, [auto]biography
/ Michelle Disler.
      p.   cm.
   ISBN 978-1-933996-25-7 (pbk. : alk. paper)
   I. Title.
PS3604.I854B66   2012
811'.6—dc23

                          2011036473

ACKNOWLEDGMENTS

I would like to thank the following mentors and friends for their encouragement and support of my work, without which this book would not be possible: Joyce Alderink, Laurel Balkema, Beverly Barrett, Josie Bloomfield, Rachel Burgess, Holly Clark, Patricia Clark, Joan Connor, JenMarie Davis, Bashak Tarkan Blanco, Lucas Blanco, Bethany Gibson Gauthier, Kimberly Hanigosky Feldkamp, Carla Harryman, Gail Heathcote, Janet Heller, Janis Butler Holm, Nick Knittel, David Lazar, Arlie Dorsch Matera, Peter Matera, Desirae Matherly, Robert Miklitsch, Jon Powers, Rachel Pridgeon Peckham, Julie Rose Platt, Jennifer Scott, Candace Stewart, Catherine Taylor, Lois Tyson, Jill Vaandering, Ed Vaandering, Wendy Wenner, and Julide Yazar. Thanks also to Ohio Wesleyan University, and to my students, whose keen interest in creative nonfiction contributes so very much to the OWU creative writing program. And sincere thanks to Tim Roberts and Julie Carr at Counterpath Press for taking a chance on my work, for which I am truly grateful.

This too for my family with love.

And with thanks to the following journals, in which portions of this book originally appeared, some in earlier forms:

Fact-Simile (*Alphabet*: "Q," "R," "Z")

Gulf Coast (*Alphabet*: "Bait," "Close Shaves," "Marriage")

Hotel Amerika (*Anatomy*: "Kiss," "Heart," "Tired")

The Laurel Review (*Alphabet*: "Approx. No. of Times," "Guide,"
"True and False"; *Anatomy*: "Drinks"; *Autobiography*
originally titled as "Lucky Number")

Painted Bride Quarterly (*Alphabet*: "Sum," "Forgetting")

Seneca Review (*Alphabet*: "Unspecified")

Witness (*Alphabet*: "Dislikes," "Hues," "Naked," "Profile,"
"Want")

FOR MY DAD

CONTENTS

No escape. There was only bluff.

IAN FLEMING

ALPHABET

APPROXIMATE NUMBER OF TIMES [BOND, JAMES]

not quite exact, ballpark   takes cold shower 10; takes ice-cold shower 1; takes sizzling cold shower 1; takes hot shower followed by cold 2; takes hot or cold bath 2; orders Bourbon 6; orders martini 10; is drunk, hung over 2; smokes 70 cigarettes per day 1; admits doesn't like killing in cold blood 7; smiles grimly [17?]; is in villain's employ 3; admits he has no plan, no way out of serious trouble 2; doubts ability to defeat villain [4?]; pumps round from gun into hotel bed or other furniture [5?]; dreams 5; sleeps dreamlessly [8?]; sleeps the "shallow sleep of ghosts and demons and screams" 1; proposes to needle villain 2; proposes 2; needles villain 8; is needled by villain [6?]; is offered a woman in marriage 1; bluffs villain [56?]; appreciates villain as a worthy adversary 6; speculates villain is completely insane [8?]; shoves gun into trouser waistband 9; says breakfast is favorite meal 3; contemplates animal beauty [taut breasts, etc.] of girl [89?]; is annoyed villain isn't more worried about him 1; cries, sobs [5?]; sneers at self for lying to girl, villain [34?]; questions gut instinct [10?]; believes in gut instinct [10?]; finds that his "heart lifts" 6; contemplates or anticipates death 5; contemplates own or another's gun [7?]; chokes back sickness, vomits or retches 7; daydreams, in sanity or delirium 4; curses lack of resolve 3; curses hubris, bravado 2; curses job 3; curses himself 1;

curses [utters unnamed profanities] 6; absolves himself, clears mind of regret [28?]; writes a poem [haiku] 1; feels, smells, or otherwise notices the "[snarling] rictus of [danger or] death" 3; is saved from a poisonous death 2; encounters cultivars of poisonous plants, fish 2; slips gun under pillow [51?]; is described as having cruel features [6?]; reflects "cheerfully" on escaping being murdered 1; is tired, exhausted 7; smells danger 1; screams 3; faints 1; groans [softly, animal, realistic, inwardly, etc.] 6; loses consciousness [89?]; wrestles with consciousness [8?]; mentally explores damage to body 6; eschews sentimental baggage 3; is ashamed 3; appreciates women who drive like men 2; endangers girl [17?]; pops amphetamines ["here's to luck"], with or without booze [5?]; "kicks his problems under the carpet of his consciousness" 1; is bored 4; writes sensitive information on paper in his own urine 1; drinks on skis while fleeing the villain 1; grips gun between his teeth 2; insists too much blood has been spilled [4?]; refuses drink 2; turns down sex 1; admits he's messed things up pretty good 3; feels "out of his depth" 1; feels no remorse 1; feels inadequate 1; is not "particularly worried by his position" 1; is "cheerfully" threatened with or contemplates death 2; is "very near to being in love" 1; is rescued by girl 4; fights squid, octopus 2; awakes to [partially or] naked girl [21?]; admits villain has total control 5; is accused of reading too many suspense novels 1; wants to give up 3; wants to survive 2; wants to die [6?]; straightens necktie upon killing villain 1; has "luncheon" with villain 4; sports with villain [golf, cards] 2; examines villain's impenetrable eyes [42?]; thinks "if only pretty girls were always angry they would be beautiful" 1; steals a kimono from a corpse to clothe his nakedness 1; is in the "grip of blood lust" 1; underestimates girl [11?]; underestimates villain [7?]; imagines girl's desirable, wet mouth [17?]; turns lesbian straight 1; speculates villain is ridiculous and extraordinary [19?]; is [threatened with or] tortured below the waist [whip, saw, bubbling hot geyser] 3; shakes hands with CIA agent and friend Felix Leiter 0

BAIT [BOND, JAMES]

temptation or lure   beautiful spies, dirty jobs on foreign shores, diamonds, death bearing down in a bottomless chair   DANGLING fast car, fast girl, fake wife, a real one, the villain's girl, anyone's girl   DANGLING selfish cars, selfish girls, selfless villains, solitary slugs on a solitary beach   DANGLING a pasty villain, a secret lair, a secret girl, a shower of flesh, cold showers, unnamed curses, voodoo curses   DANGLING amphetamines, exposed throats, bloodlust, breathy moans, balls for the job, bachelorhood, wedded bliss, bourbon, boredom   DANGLING firm breasts and tight bottoms   DANGLING the villain's peccadilloes

CLOSE SHAVES, SCRAPES [BOND, JAMES]

escape . . . respiratory paralysis induced by *fugu* poison from sex organs of Japanese globe-fish; poisonous tropical centipede crawling up the "warm forest" of the groin: "Supposing it liked the warmth there! Supposing it tried to crawl into the crevices! Could [007] stand it? Supposing it chose to bite!"; assault course of death measuring anatomy of courage and will to survive the killing ground as includes battle with life-size man-eating squid; "pain" from the Latin *poena* and the gleaming teeth of a circular saw pointed at [007's] feet and groin; forced employ in burgling Fort Knox; SMERSH executioner's carefully planned ruin of 007 on board Orient Express: "'It'll give me an extra kick telling the famous Mister Bond of the Secret Service what a bloody fool he is. You see, old man, you're not so good as you think. You're a stuffed dummy and I've been given the job of letting the sawdust out of you'"; Comrade Rosa Klebb's deadly knitting needles and knife-toed shoe; "Death Warrant made out in the name of James Bond. Description: *Angliski Spion*. Crime: Enemy of the [Soviet] State"; Dreamy Pines Motor Lodge American mob-driven motel fire: "There was a crash and a great shower of sparks way down the line of cabins. James Bond said, 'There goes my shirt. Roof falling in on top of it.' He paused to wipe his hand down his dirty sweating face so that the black smudged even worse. 'I had a feeling that was going to happen'"; camaraderie in the Mediterranean with a friendly piratical smuggler, a thief to catch a thief: "'Ah, the quiet Englishman. He fears nothing save the emotions!'"; probationary crook in American mob-driven smuggling ring, rescued by tough-talking diamond smuggling broad after taking a beating: "Bond heard the two guards come up behind him. 'Take him out on the platform,' said Mr Spang. Bond saw the corner of his tongue come out and slightly tough the thin lips. 'Brooklyn Stomping. Eighty Percenter. 'Kay?'"; shoving off from simulated Old Western desert tableaux town during which time 007 finds between his wounds and the desert action that he's delirious; staged post-duel murder-suicide of "pretty" Spangled mobsters aboard getaway cruise ship: "The quiet bullet and the quiet knife crossed in mid-air, and the eyes of the two men flinched simultaneously as the weapons struck. But the flinch in the eyes of the fat man turned into an upward roll of the eyeballs as he fell backwards, clawing at his heart, while Bond's eyes only looked incuriously down at the spreading stain on his shirt and at the flat handle of the knife hanging loosely from its folds"; dazed and newly wed 007 en route to honeymoon with dead wife: "Bond put his arm around her shoulders across which the dark patches had begun to flower. He pressed her against him. 'It's all right,' he said in a clear voice as if explaining something to a child. 'It's quite all right. She's having a rest. We'll be going on soon. There's no hurry. You see—' Bond's head sank down against hers and he whispered into her hair—'you see, we've got all the time in the world'"

DISLIKES [BOND, JAMES]

hates, displays aversion to   double-agent girlfriend ALSO
dirty jobs, women drivers, women spies, poisonous fish, poisonous
insects, poisonous plants, egomaniacs ALSO   villains who touch
his gun, sodden guns, hired guns ALSO   peace, panic, henchmen,
genital mutilation, losing at cards, restraint, flowers ALSO   cry-
ing in double bourbons, in airport bars, cheaters, prudes, li-
ars ALSO   helpless women, women of privilege, women who are
overly made up, unattractive women ALSO   Barracudas ALSO
being held hostage, vague death threats, whispers of death, the smell
of danger, desk jobs ALSO   thieves, murderers, assassins, gang-
sters, sticklers ALSO   fear, feelings of inadequacy ALSO   killing
in cold blood, spilling too much blood, bloodlust ALSO   displays
of arrogance, missing breakfast, being spied on ALSO   greedy vil-
lains, stupid villains, fleshy villains, American villains, ex-patriot
villains, easy villains, titled philanthropic villains ALSO   dowries,
duplicity, disguises, disclosure, death ALSO   boredom, sentiment,
long seductions, "pimping for England" ALSO   kidnapping, ki-
monos ALSO   rejection, excuses, bad dreams, bad judgment,
bad food, bad bets, bad blood ALSO   memories, marriage, mis-
ery, remorse, the occult ALSO   depression, vertigo, vomiting, *vin
triste* ALSO   loss of a loved one, losing ALSO   self-loathing

EPIGRAPH [BOND, JAMES]

"Bond peered through the slits in his mask. Yes, by God! Two of the thugs were standing beside the ticket man watching the throng with deadly concentration. On the far side of the road stood the black Mercedes, petrol vapour curling up from its exhaust. No escape. There was only bluff. Bond put his arm around Tracy's neck and whispered, 'Kiss me all the way past the ticket table. They're there, but I think we can make it.'

She flung an arm over his shoulder and drew him near to her. 'How did you know that that's what I've been waiting for?'"

"Fork Lift for Hell!"
On Her Majesty's Secret Service
Ian Fleming 1963

FORGETTING [BOND, JAMES]

contingent, like acts of mastery, on   beauty, champagne, empty
magazine, loaded magazine, rare blood type, her broken nose, kill-
ing in cold blood, license to kill, limits to a man's courage   ON TOP
OF   death-cure, voodoo curse, vomiting on the beach, violet hour,
velvet dress drawn tightly across the breasts, the saying of unpleas-
ant things   AS WELL AS   shark repellent, sleep of dreams, small
curling waves inside the reef on a foreign shore, slight tingling of
the scalp, scent in the nose of a clean sea, nightmares, non-essential
parts of the body, bamboo shade along the sweltering banks, beach
sand littered with bullets   ADDED TO   holiday in the sun, hypoc-
risy toward her, hot silence, hard sand too warm for sleep, "Why do
they hate us so much," sweeping waves of sleep, "Would you like
me in white with pale blue birds flying over me," phantom mem-
ories, manacled wrists, memory of pain, illusion of power,   "pair
of queens kiss[ing] the green cloth," her glittering body, her body
torn lifeless from the churning sea   OVER AND ABOVE   swirl of
movement in dark glass, sass, soft mission, standing transfixed, slight
flush at the temples, "the sensual bluntness that breeds mistakes,"
too much champagne, too many cold showers, too much blood, a
terribly exciting girl, colored glass, gone soft on account of poisoned
fruit, gone pale   WITH   clenched teeth, cruel eyes, unnamed curses,

gun-sight ground into the coccyx, grated egg with caviar, skeleton grip, imagination above everything else PLUS empty window frames, expensive pine-bath essences, questions as easy as possible, the vital purpose of evil, peccadilloes, "privileged to emerge better and more virtuous men"

GUIDE [BOND, JAMES]

words commonly used in this work, an index of

Amphetamines, 3, 27, 31, 32
Animal, 3, 4, 13
Avalanche, 31, 32

Beach, 4, 8, 12, 19, 20, 26, 31
Bed, bedroom, etc., 3, 4, 12, 13, 17,
    18, 19, 20, 21, 28, 31
Benzedrine, 4, 18
Bird shit, 15, 31
Bitch, bitchily, etc., 4, 12, 13, 30
Blind faith, 4, 13, 31
Blood, bloody, bloodlust, etc., 3, 4, 6,
    8, 12, 13, 15, 17, 18, 20, 30, 32,
    33, 34, 35
Bluff, 3, 4, 7, 13, 20, 22, 28, 30, 31
Bourbon, 3, 4, 6, 18, 22, 26, 30, 32
Bravado, 3, 30
Breakfast, 3, 4, 6, 12, 20, 22, 30, 34
Breasts, 3, 4, 8, 12, 18, 22, 27
Bullet, 4, 5, 8, 15, 18, 21, 26, 30, 32

Casino, 4, 27, 31
Chair, 4, 22, 26, 31
Champagne, 8, 22, 27, 30, 32, 35
Conscience, 18, 20, 22, 26, 31
Consciousness, unconsciousness, etc.,
    3, 13, 17, 30, 31

Cruel, cruelty, etc., 3, 8, 15, 17, 18, 20,
    22, 26
Curses, 3, 4, 8, 13

Danger, dangerous, endanger, etc., 3, 6,
    12, 13, 18, 26, 30, 31
Death, dead, deadly, die, etc., 3, 4, 5, 6,
    7, 8, 12, 13, 15, 16, 18, 19, 20, 21,
    22, 23, 26, 27, 29, 30, 31, 32
Death garden, 4, 12, 31
Desire, 18, 19, 25
Double agent girlfriend, 6, 16, 18, 22,
    26, 32, 34, 36
Dream, dreamlessly, sweet dreams,
    dreaming, etc., 3, 4, 5, 6, 8, 19,
    30, 31

Escape, escaping, etc., 4, 5, 7, 19, 21,
    27, 30, 31, 32
Eyes, 3, 4, 5, 8, 12, 13, 18, 22, 26, 32,
    33, 34

Gold, golden, etc., 12, 13, 15, 20, 22,
    24, 24, 30, 31, 33
Girl, 3, 4, 8, 12, 13, 15, 17, 19, 20, 21,
    26, 27, 28, 29, 31, 33, 35
Green, 8, 12, 30, 31

Groan, 3, 13
Groin, 4, 5, 12, 13
Gun, gunshot, etc., 3, 4, 6, 12, 13, 15,
    19, 20, 22, 28, 31, 32, 24
Gut, gut instinct, etc., 3, 13, 21, 22,
    26, 31

Harpoon, 15, 16

Insect, 6, 13, 15

Kidnapping, 6, 16, 22
Kill, killed, killing, etc., 3, 4, 5, 6, 8,
    13, 15, 16, 18, 20, 21, 22, 26, 27
Kimono, 3, 6, 12, 13
Kiss, 4, 7, 8, 23, 33

Lavender, 8, 12
Lips, 3, 5, 12, 23, 32
Love, 3, 4, 5, 6, 13, 15, 18, 19, 20, 21,
    22, 30, 33
Luck, 3, 13, 27, 30

Martini, 3, 20, 22, 26, 30, 32
Marry, marriage, etc., 3, 4, 6, 15, 18,
    19, 22, 26, 27, 30, 34
Missile, 12, 14, 15, 20, 26, 34
Moon, moonlight, honeymoon, etc., 4,
    5, 12, 18, 30, 31, 32
Murder, 5, 6, 15, 16
Mutilation, 6, 22

Naked, nakedness, etc., 3, 4, 13, 19,
    20, 26

Neck, 4, 7, 13, 15

Pain, 5, 8, 12, 13, 18, 31
Pill, 15, 18, 20, 30, 31
Poison, poisoned, poisonous, etc., 3, 4,
    5, 6, 12, 14, 15, 33

Resolve, 3, 20, 26, 27, 31

Sea, 4, 5, 8, 12, 13, 15, 24, 31, 32
Selfish, 26, 33
Sex, sexy, sexual, etc., 3, 5, 13, 16, 20,
    22, 25, 26, 27
Shower, 3, 4, 5, 8, 13, 19, 20, 22
Smuggled, smuggling, etc, 5, 24, 32, 36
Soul, 13, 18, 22, 30, 32
Suffocation, 15
Suicide, 15, 16, 18, 20, 34, 36

Tender, 28
Tentacles, 12, 30
Tragic, 28

Villain, 3, 4, 6, 13, 15, 16, 18, 19, 20,
    21, 22, 25, 26, 27, 28, 29, 30, 31,
    32, 33
Vodka, 12, 22, 30
Vomit, vomiting, etc., 3, 6, 13, 19
Voodoo, 8, 15, 17, 18, 34

Wife, 5, 20, 21, 3

HUES [BOND, JAMES]

spectrum, shade   BLACK   blood in the moonlight, coffee to the brim, crabs nibbling at limbs in the rising tide, marmalade, memories, moonlit shadows on a bedroom wall, pepper to sink the impurities, piratical eye patch, satin tuxedo tie, shimmering tunnel of pain, "solid river of birds," triangle between her legs, one tightly stretched velvet dress   BLUE   beret, blowtorch flame, camera bomb, empty sky, gazing orbs, grim face in the dashboard light, worsted wool trousers   BROWN   bloodstained floorboards, bloodstained sea, poisonous centipedes, fresh speckled eggs for breakfast   GREEN   boring orbs obscured by tinted lenses, gaming tables the color of "grass on a fresh tomb"   GREY   ashen faces, boiling mud bubbling up underneath the groin, carpet under a dead man's bed, thin lips   GUNMETAL   cigarette box, shimmering ki-mono   LAVENDER   breath, poisonous blossoms, trousers with a chocolate shirt   PINK   nesting birds, death garden dragonflies, finest *foie gras*, satin brassiere and old fashioned knickers, shark eyes, scuttling crab-like hands, scattered shells, shocking scarf tied round the hair, small clouds, small waves at sunrise, the spray of flesh   PURPLE   poisonous fruit, tentacle snaking up the leg in the sea   RED   blazing eyes in a blood drained face, bushy mous-tache, full and open lips, lamp shades, a mist of pain, a petulant face, top secret telephone, trail of bloody footprints, vivid streak across left cheek and bridge of the nose VIOLET dusk, restaurant menus, a girl's name, scented breath for the saying of unpleasant things BONE-WHITE beach, moonlight MILK-WHITE missile dome, teeth WHITE chicken feather, corners of the mouth, dregs in the bottom of an empty glass, linen bathing drawers, shaking hands, heavy snow, terror YELLOW cold eyes, commanding eyes, dim bulbs of marsh buggies, gambling chips, butter on breakfast toast, warm lights, small flames, poisonous centipedes, wide eyes in a zombie-like face

ITEM [BOND, JAMES]

entry, accounting of   ITEM   disrobes on command for imma-
nent torture, sex ITEM   lies, lays with eyes closed ITEM   ten-
ders resignation, kills resignedly ITEM   waits for pain, reels from
pain, is revived by pain ITEM   destroys sniper without killing
her ITEM   kicks problems "under the carpet of his conscious-
ness" ITEM   welcomes the velvet heat ITEM   fears long, flat,
brown poisonous insects ITEM   hurls crabs into mangrove, sleeps
soundly on the warm sand, awakes lazily ITEM   sings island tune
with half-naked shell-collecting girl ITEM   wonders how well
waterlogged gun will shoot ITEM   gets "poor little bitch" into a
bit of a mess ITEM   responds instinctually to girl's warm "animal"
smell, beauty ITEM   responds instinctually to girl, villain's wildly
improbable story of horror, hardship ITEM   responds instinctually
to immanent sex, death and disrobes, lies, or groans ITEM   curses,
flirts with girl, danger for work, play, sport ITEM   squeezes
her hand, lies to her face, curses her ignorance ITEM   rescues
her rescuing him ITEM   drops, hides, shoves gun under pillow,
in waistband ITEM   feigns love, hate, indifference for world
peace, untold pleasure ITEM   curses bad luck, failed gut when
bound, bound for death at sea, on land ITEM   staggers, vom-
its having been drugged, showered with blood ITEM   covets,

curses kimono for clothing nakedness ITEM dines, drinks with girl, villain, freely, under duress ITEM sips thoughtfully, bluffs thinly, shamelessly with girl, villain, over dinner and drinks, before and after sex, torture ITEM imagines strangling villain with relish, relief ITEM gazes vaguely, disrobes moodily, fatalistically ITEM is mistaken by girl for villain, mistakes girl for villain, mistakes villain for a girl ITEM hears nothing but the sound of their feet as they flee ITEM brandishes warm gun, opens strange doors ITEM leaves, loves careful, careless women in bed, on job ITEM recoils, recovers from exhaustion, injury ITEM admires, curses girl's willingness, resolve ITEM admits, approves hypocrisy, happenstance ITEM counts hours, minutes, seconds to deliverance, death, at sea, on board train, underground, under the sea, on a tram, in the bedroom ITEM saves, loses girls, villains, weapons ITEM attracts, abandons girls, villains, weapons ITEM loves, leaves girls, villains, weapons ITEM eschews safe girls, loose weapons ITEM delivers death with gun without panic ITEM rues, romances girl, mission ITEM considers morosely, resignedly drowning thoughts, girl, thoughts of girl ITEM reaches for, tortured by girl, villain, suddenly, shamelessly ITEM slips arms around girl, villain's neck with relish, pleasure, revenge, passion ITEM considers caliber of girl, gun, villain ITEM feels balance, blind faith going fast

J SOLVE FOR UNNAMED VARIABLES [BOND, JAMES]

j = "point of etiquette" (unnamed) e, b

j = poisonous evergreens (suicide) n, l

j = nuclear missiles (stolen) x, z

KILLING [BOND, JAMES]

moment or act of, a survey of

How many guns, hands, knives, swords, bullets have you aimed,
    spent, used, wielded? How many failed attempts?
How many unplanned or unexplained?
How many covered up or uncovered?
How many too soon or not soon enough?
How many above or below sea level?

Of those unplanned or unexpected, how many were beneficial,
    negligible, or sad?
Of those flawlessly executed, which were pleasurable, bloody,
    beautiful, or banal?
Of those involving poisonous plants or insects, which were
    doomed to fail?

Which deaths were guaranteed successes or lacking in originality?

When do you stop killing—on feeling sympathy for the villain,
    yourself, or the double agent girlfriend whose suicide took
    you by surprise?

Assuming you've shot, strangled, harpooned, derailed, blown up
    or drowned every last traitorous double agent, murderous
    assassin, and shadowy villain, would there be any death left
    over, any you wish you could share with anyone else?

Who was dead already?

L SOLVE FOR UNNAMED VARIABLES [BOND, JAMES]

l = black widow spider (exotic) y, k
l = voodoo drums (thunderous) r, n
l = Istanbul (exotic) x, n

MARRIAGE [BOND, JAMES]

cliché . . . that Ian Fleming's 007 considers marriage may actually be more surprising than the number of 007's self-identified "untidy affairs," given that 007's work demands he sacrifice himself in ways more violent and aggressive for world security, and given how close and how often are these compromising positions in which 007 finds himself. While taking a nature cure at a private and silent non-smoking clinic, 007 was stretched hard and long on a rack, a device designed for stretching the spine, but which, once Bond was tied down, had, in the wrong hands, the capacity for doing a good body great harm. A device for healing in the villain's hands had become a more dangerous cure. And Bond might as well be married to this risky business of spying to save the world, tied forever to a fantasy of security not even he can always enforce. Either way, 007's fit to be tied to the perils of pain and pleasure, stretched on the rack of social and villainous ills and wills, hopped up on Benzedrine, Bourbon, and Babes. He could be tied down because he's married to evil by way of his desire for the good; because he needs a good threat, a hard tug at his conscience wearied by ambivalence over killing in cold blood; because he needs resistance like the world needs a cure for every last one of its own untidy affairs. Bond is before long so knotted up body and soul with the cares of the world and his own small desires that he winds up the victim of circumstance like the kind that nearly ripped him limb from handsome limb. He could be tied down, promise love and fidelity. Why is that so hard to believe? Why is it a stretch, like the promise of a villain reformed, this spy trading in his world-saving ways for wedded bliss? Torture, mortality, a spy's life compromised, its pleasures and perils given up like chastity for bliss like the kind that's wedded to domesticity? But sweet mother of all things diabolical, the sacrifice marriage would mean for Bond is almost ritualistic, a villain's fantasy, demanding the kind of compromise so costly evil could beget evil in practically no time, no time at all. In less time than it takes Bond to say "I do," Mrs. Bond winds up dead, blood blooming on her shirt en route to their honeymoon while she lies face down in the steering wheel, killed by a bullet meant for Bond. And before Mrs. Bond, Vesper, a darling double agent Bond would have married, but whose suicide by overdose of sleeping pills was her only means to an honorable end, because she couldn't "bear the look in [Bond's] dear eyes." It's a crowded bed for Bond, comfortless, racked with nuptial guilt barely veiled like the figure of Mrs. Bond whose breasts appear on the novel's cover like the twin snow capped firs and mountain peaks over which 007 skis, flees to safety.

NAKED [BOND, JAMES]

denuded, exposed   without remorse NAKED   without dis-
guise NAKED   without help on foreign shores NAKED   without
a good hand NAKED   under the cool sheets NAKED   bleeding
in a bottomless chair NAKED   dreaming the sleep of dreams NA-
KED   considering marriage on an empty beach NAKED   es-
caping death NAKED   downing uppers NAKED   swimming,
vomiting NAKED   promising vengeance and death NAKED   if
not for stolen or borrowed clothing NAKED   in a stone-cold
shower NAKED   with a stone cold girl NAKED   in a grass hut
on the beach NAKED   in the room next door NAKED   in the
perfumed bath she drew for him NAKED   in the villain's spare
room with a spare girl NAKED   on the velvety island breeze NA-
KED   stripped at cards, without hard currency NAKED   except
for cigarettes and a stolen kimono NAKED   except for his objec-
tions and desires NAKED   once the mission is over with a ciga-
rette afterward NAKED   without a gun or a girl in the world

OBJECTIONS [BOND, JAMES]

in the form of twenty questions for   How many times do you think you've nearly bought it on account of a girl? What would your mother say, if she were alive, about the number of notches in your bedpost—Vesper, Tatiana, the Masterson sisters, one of whom wound up dead, suffocated in gold paint because of you—their numbers like spent shell casings in a little black book of your psychosexual secrets?

Bluffing villains over dinner in their fortified lairs, tagging along half-naked girls you just happen to meet on the beach—with your gun tucked into the waistband of your trousers all the while? Cold showers : seventy cigarettes a day : a fight to the death with a giant man-eating squid : Is this what you think it means to work like you don't need the money, love like you've never been hurt?

This next question may sound a little naïve, but how is it you don't often have a plan for getting your fool ass out of all those really tight spots—*I know, I know* a spy can't always plan these things, a spy learns to adapt—or rather, diabolical plans for world domination aside, how do you get your fool ass into the oddest kinds of fixes: your prolonged battle for survival in Dr. No's Obstacle

Course of Death comes to mind, which is right up there with being strong-armed into burgling Fort Knox with Goldfinger who was determined to have the world's only gold supply. Keep your friends close, your enemies closer? Who snorkels for the villain's hidden nuclear missiles and makes mad love to the villain's girl on the beach—well, I guess *that* one make sense, but have you ever really considered what it means to go after another man's missiles, or to engage in extended meditations, reveries on your own or another's gun, in psychoanalytic circles?

Who asks the villain's girl to spy on her illustrious boyfriend, knowing all too well certain death upon discovery is her cruel reward? What kind of meals do villains serve when the tables are turned and they serve you your impending demise like the stiff drinks you always order at the silliest, worst times? When you named your favorite martini The Vesper after your first lady love in the novels, did you cast the name out like the suicide note Vesper left behind, confessing her love and her duplicity?

You're a spy—the world's best—how did you not know, until you'd planned to make her your wife, Vesper was a double agent? How are you not dead like the girls who wind up loving you, their resolve weak, glittering like the dresses you peel from their bodies like skin from a ripe tropical fruit? How am I doing? Do you think I'm finished? Do you think you deserve a break after all that saving the world, one hard-won villain's death, one tragically oversexed girl at a time?

Do you really not like killing in cold blood? You say so at least once in every novel, and it begins to read like a public service announcement, almost like you're telling reader and villain alike *This is going to hurt me more than it'll hurt you*, which is nice, but do you think we believe you? Look at you—"martinis, girls, and guns" might as well be your middle name. You have "sex for dinner, death for breakfast" and the small white scar on your cheek reads like one hell of a short lifeline you've extended every year since 1953 when Fleming gave you life in prose, or since 1962 at the very least, when the world began immortalizing you on the silver screen. You haven't really aged a day? And while we're still here, what about the women you've failed to protect—your wife took a bullet meant for you, I'm sure you'll recall—and the villains who've escaped you—a guy in your line of work doesn't get fired for that kind of thing?

The villain runs free to challenge the world again, and all you've got to show for it are busty brainless girls who ask "You *do* love me a little bit don't you?" while M wants to know "What the devil's going on"? Good thing the movies smoothed out the hiccups in the novels, made you more certain, less human, especially when it's all our asses on the line if you don't save the day. We'd all die. You want that on your conscience? Do you have one? You're like the villains you kill, the girls you go to bed with—all of them determined to win, to be the marvelous, sparkling world prize worth fighting for.

Maybe we end here—I feel like that's something a villain might say, only with him there'd be no "maybe" : "We end here, Mister Bond," he'd say as he left you in the clutches of some ridiculous machine, to die—and equally ridiculous, isn't it, how we hope for your impossible escape every last time? Which makes me wonder, as I picture you near death with a sweaty furrowed brow and cursing your gut that's failed you for the last time—how do you expect to live, 007? How do you expect to die?

PROFILE [BOND, JAMES]

anon.   travels under pseudonyms but without disguise; possessing terrific gut instinct; possessing cold, cruel features including eyes, mouth, and white scar on right cheek; drinks bourbon; drinks vodka martinis with a lemon peel in champagne glasses; smokes 70 gold ringed special blend cigarettes per day; sleeps with preferred gun under pillow; wears gun in trouser waistband, but has been known to clench it between his teeth when situation demands he have his hands free; prefers cold showers and colder women, including but not limited to, tight breasted, firm bottomed double agents, enemy agents, free agents, and naturalists; baits and bluffs villains over dinner and sport with surprising failure and uncanny success; suffers inexplicable torture of body and absurd manipulation of mind when he's not careful; finds no shortage of ways for getting firm breasted, tight bottomed double agents, enemy agents, free agents, and naturalists, sometimes belonging to villain, into and out of the kinds of trouble most often associated with kidnapping, torture, and death; finds no shortage of ways for getting himself into trouble most often associated with mutilation, poisoning, and localized personal injury, often on account of kidnapped or tortured double agents, enemy agents, free agents, and naturalists; prefers anonymity; prefers breakfast as favorite meal of the day;

has feigned marriage to naturalists and enemy agents as situation requires; has believed himself in love with and proposed marriage to double and enemy agents; an expert marksman who believes "a live target needs another kind of nerve"; handsome as the day is long; only rarely drunk on booze and a dirty job; he is most often weighed down by the conscience of the world

Q SOLVE FOR UNNAMED VARIABLES [BOND, JAMES]

q = death threats (hot, deadly) s, w
q = bubbling mud bath (hot, deadly) x, n
q = lips for kissing (hot, deadly) a, z
q = "pimping for England" (hot, deadly) r, s
q = whisky (vague) y, n

R SOLVE FOR UNNAMED VARIABLES [BOND, JAMES]

r = evil on a calm sea (tight, shiny) a, c

r = black satin stockings (tight, shiny) m, p

r = "I admit I've fallen for her" (tight, shiny) l, n

r = smuggling diamonds (tight, shiny) s, q

SUM [BOND, JAMES]

desire, economy of   a real romantic rule   OR   without stan-
dard mathematical deviation, which encompasses occurrences
falling from the average or the norm   OR   point values assigned
for current romantic prospects   OR   sexual currency   OR   "the
combined total amount of anything"

[CASE, TIFFANY 50] + [BOND, JAMES – 19]   = 31 / 24 [chapters to
climax, inevitable lights out for cartoonish American gangsters] =
1.29 / 5.0 scale = 26% compatibility

[DI VICENZO, TRACY 45] + [BOND, JAMES 42] = 87 / 27 [chapters
to climax, inevitable lights out for Mrs. Cmdr. Bond] = 3.22 / 5.0
scale = 64% compatibility

[LYND, VESPER 19] + [BOND, JAMES 34] = 53 / 27 [chapters to cli-
max, inevitable lights out for double agent girlfriend] = 1.96 / 5.0
scale = 39% compatibility

[ROMANOVA, TATIANA 32] + [BOND, JAMES – 17)] = 15 / 28 [chapters
to climax, inevitable lights out for Bond] = .535 / 5.0 scale = 11%
compatibility

[VITALI, DOMINO 31] + [BOND, JAMES 23] = 54 / 24 [chapters to climax, inevitable lights out for villainous boyfriend] = 2.25 / 5.0 scale = 45% compatibility

TRUE OR FALSE [BOND, JAMES]

_____ James Bond likes girls who make him feel like an expensive gigolo on holiday.

_____ James Bond has never liked "pimping for England."

_____ James Bond agrees: martinis are good, but a double bourbon is better.

_____ For James Bond, life is death, and death is strangely sexy. Sex is usually just sex, unless the girl dies. Then sex is death again.

_____ James Bond must always concern himself with whether or not the villain takes him seriously, and the villain must always concern himself with anything, anything at all.

_____ There's only one thing James Bond likes more than selfish women, whose resolve he likes to shatter, roughly, and that's a selfish car.

_____ James Bond only steals the villain's girlfriend when the villain isn't looking. If the villain is looking, James Bond knows his cruel features, specifically, his cold grey-blue eyes and the small white scar on his right cheek, will do the work for him. But sometimes the girl and her villain-boyfriend both fall for James Bond when James Bond is especially reckless with his reckless good looks.

_____ James Bond trusts his infallible gut whenever possible, except when it's not possible, and then he shoves his warm gun into the waistband of his trousers, pushes back the hair from his forehead, and utters a string of unnamed profanities, which ends in his cursing his gut for failing to alert him to such dangerous prospects. How could he not have known?

_____ There are times when James Bond has been beaten or tortured, almost to death. This is when he wishes death would surprise him with kindness, not cruelty.

_____ When James Bond gets naked on the beach, goes for a swim, and thinks of proposing marriage to his girl, he's only disappointed there's no one there to see him.

_____ Though he would never publicly admit it, James Bond routinely absolves himself and the villain of wrongdoing. "The Devil has a rotten time," he says, "and I always like to be on the side of the underdog. We don't give the poor chap a chance."

_____ Only a selfish woman could make James Bond give up a selfish car.

_____ Only a selfish car could make James Bond give up a selfish woman.

_____ James Bond appreciates women who drive like men, champagne perfectly chilled with crushed amphetamines, and smiling grimly in the dusky blue evening light outside casinos on foreign shores. He dislikes women who drive like women, ugly women, tight women, and women who forgo wearing dresses stretched tightly across their breasts, though he has made exceptions for the occasional prude whose resolve he has found appealing.

_____ James Bond will marry you should you lose at cards, but you must be a woman with a fast white car and a knowledge of racing tires.

_____ James Bond will marry you if you're the most expensive sex he's ever had with a reckless woman. But you'd have to tell him to go to hell first.

_____ James Bond doesn't believe in luck.

_____ James Bond believes luck is a woman.

_____ James Bond believes "luck in all its moods ha[s] to be loved, not feared."

_____ You'd be lucky if James Bond loved you.

_____ You could be Bond's "darling" if you're a double agent who kills herself before he can marry you, because nothing puts the screws to James Bond like a girl he can't rescue or a villain he can't kill, especially when they're the same person.

_____ James Bond is a walking death warrant, reflecting cheerfully on his repeated and narrow escapes from death as flesh rains down from the sky.

UNSPECIFIED [BOND, JAMES]

absurd categories, an index of

See also Most Ridiculous Utterance by a Girl in Bed

Bond's Best Resignation Attempt. *See also* Most Ridiculous Utterance by a Girl in Bed

Bond's Most Masturbatory Moment. *See also* Bond's Most Compelling Meditation on Gun

Bond's Most Ridiculous Utterance. *See also* Most Ridiculous Utterance by a Girl in Bed

Bond's Oddest Most Compelling Meditation on Girl. *See also* Bond's Most Compelling Meditation on Gun

Bond's Oddest Most Compelling Meditation on Gun. *See also* Bond's Most Compelling Meditation on Girl

Bond's Worst Judgment Call. *See also* Bond's Best White Knight Moment

Bond's Best White Knight Moment. *See also* Most Ridiculous Utterance by a Girl in Bed

Girl Bond Most or Least Resembles. *See also* Most or Least Complicated Girl

Least Surprising Death of Girl. *See also* Most Complicated Girl

Most Complicated Girl. *See also* Most Complicated Mission

Most Complicated Mission. *See also* Most Complicated Girl

Most Complicated Villain. *See also* Best Girl; Best Bond

Most Ridiculous Utterance by a Girl. *See also* Most Ridiculous Utterance by a Girl in Bed

Most Ridiculous Utterance by a Girl in Bed. *See also* Most Ridiculous Utterance by a Girl; Most Ridiculous Utterance by a Girl in Bed

Trickiest Most Duplicitous Most Underestimated Girl. *See also* Worst Bond

Villain Bond Most or Least Resembles. *See also* Best Girl

Villain Most Likely to Succeed. *See also* Best Girl

Villain's Least Convincing Tough Guy Moment. *See also* Best Girl

Villain's Most Ridiculous Utterance. *See also* Most Ridiculous Utterance by a Girl

Worst Bond. *See also* Best Girl; Most Ridiculous Utterance by a Girl in Bed

Worst Rescue by a Girl. *See also* Most Ridiculous Utterance by a Girl; Most Ridiculous Utterance by a Girl in Bed; Villain Most Likely to Succeed

Worst Villain. *See also* Best Girl

Worst Villain to Work For. *See also* Girl Most Likely to Succeed

VANISHED [BOND, JAMES]

cease, fade away   memory, marriage, mangroves, millions, poor little bitches, bomb-throwers in straw hats, bachelorhood, Beretta, bullets, peace, pale primrose moon, petrol, a small carafe of vodka very cold, a mouthful of muscle at the shoulder, great luxury, luck, lethargy, last evenings, calling card on a timer switch, the last few years, the last few villains, Vesper, foolishness, steady flame, old flame, a few hazy details, courage, consciousness, concentration, snow capped peaks, ash, anonymity, an average hand, "all the time in the world," hubris, escape, easy dreamless sleep, sleeping pills, pleasant proportions, pain lines, disguises, dry martinis in deep glasses, dinner, death, dragons, dignity, dreams, screams, swimming trunks, languor, a loaded magazine, indifference, amphetamines and whole bottles of champagne, goodness, gold, diamonds, more diamonds, cigarette case, Tiffany Case, tranquillizers, freedom, four letter words, Solitaire, shame, saliva, all sensation, sight, slimy tentacles, cigarettes, secrets, his senses and his wits, one whisky and soda too many, small precautions, concealment, breakfast, bravado, bourbon, backup, buried treasure, balance, boredom, resignation, regret, reverence, recognition, worry, wonder, wife, bloodstained lips, sinking ships, souls, seconds, minutes, breath, drums enough to wake all Jamaica

WANT [BOND, JAMES]

to feel the lack of   I want to be your smoking gun. I want to be your stolen bar of gold. I want to be your golden girl, priceless and inestimable, but not dead on the bed like the last one. I want to be your gut instinct, solid and riddled with holes the size of Texas. Whose gut would I be otherwise? I want to be your inky black octopus in the churning sea, reaching for the flailing, failing body of its subterranean dreams. I want to be your only means of escape, close, narrow, improbable, stowed on board getaway cruise ship, railcar, car, and floating, coasting, racing away from villains partially destroyed, always deformed, sometimes escaped, which means I would have to be your villain, too, but not dead under a pile of bird shit, not dead in the death garden of my own design but escaped, in a swirling, icy cloud of snow, an avalanche the size of Texas, which means I would have to be your avalanche, too, pure and white, glistening by the pale moon so you can see your way, but only sometimes. I want to be your alligator-skin billfold. I want to be your solitary, not the girl who reads the cards—that's *Solitaire*—solitary, the moment before a mission when you're alone on the beach with only a nip, a long pull, a slug, and your gun, amphetamines, and conscience to guide you. Solitary. Whose beverage or bitter pill would I be otherwise? I want to be your glinting pale moon squinting through window blinds, your flinty resolve, your blind faith, misplaced and reckless, hopeless, careless, feckless. Sometimes. I may as well be the smooth dice you roll with the flick of a steady wrist over the grass-green baize in a sweaty, smoke-filled casino with odds like yours. I'll be your danger, too, with all the rights and privileges afforded by danger to a person in your position, which is most often the blessed unconsciousness that comes with the pain of being tortured in bottomless chairs by so many megalomaniacs. This is when I'd want to be your bluff however thin, the shoulder shrug that says you don't know how you made such a mess of things. You don't know how you're going to get out of it. But these things have a way of working themselves out, because villains succumb every day to their own ruthless, ill-fated designs—spies, too—and when the chips are down, I would be your cheerful escape from death, the brave words sounding hollowly in your mouth.

X VARIABLE [BOND, JAMES]

if then solve for

death warrant (signed) *s*
death threats (vague) *q*
black widow spider (exotic) *l*
moonlight (dusky) *k*
trees (bloody) *y*
escape on skis (avalanche) *z*
champagne (too much, not enough) *y*
spinning circular saw *w*
whisky (vague) *q*
bullets (on the beach) *p*
crushed amphetamines *e*
"point of etiquette" (unnamed) *j*
"She says she's in love with you" (exotic) *b*
knitting needles (deadly) *x*
bubbling mud bath (hot, deadly) *q*
table knife (hidden) *n*
shark repellent *p*
lips for kissing (hot, deadly) *q*
underwater cave ("treasure hunt") *z*

bag of golf clubs ("treasure hunt") *b*
stolen bars of gold ("treasure hunt") *s*
poisonous evergreens (suicide) *j*
Istanbul (exotic) *l*
drowning thoughts *n*
drowning girl *t*
tight velvet dress *p*
non-essential body parts *m*
bamboo on the banks *n*
suicide note ("the bitch is dead") *z*
proposing marriage ("the bitch is dead") *x*
red telephone (top secret) *y*
dark glittering eyes *m*
tight glittering dress *n*
"Women are for recreation" ("the bitch is dead") *x*
double agent ("the bitch is dead") *z*
voodoo drums (thunderous) *l*
"I admit I've fallen for her" (express train) *r*
girl on the "gun-arm" ("suicide")

Y SOLVE FOR UNNAMED VARIABLES [BOND, JAMES]

y = double agent (lure) z, n

y = trees (bloody) l, k

y = red telephone (top secret) z, x

y = "Was he getting serious about this girl?" (express train) p, w

y = "We'll get plenty of sleep in the grave" (Vegas) z, b

y = champagne (too much, not enough) z, w

Z SOLVE FOR UNNAMED VARIABLES [BOND, JAMES]

z = diamond smuggler ("treasure hunt") y, n

z = escape on skis (avalanche) y, w

z = suicide note ("the bitch is dead") x, y

z = underwater cave ("treasure hunt") y, b

z = double agent ("the bitch is dead") j, x

ANATOMY

CIGARETTES [BOND, JAMES]

(The action: *smoking*, 1953–1965, 1966)

James Bond took out a cigarette and lit it.[1]
James Bond lit a cigarette.
James Bond lit a cigarette.
James Bond lit a cigarette.
James Bond lit a cigarette.
James Bond lit a cigarette.
James Bond lit a cigarette.
James Bond lit a cigarette.
James Bond lit a cigarette.
James Bond lit a cigarette.
James Bond lit a cigarette.
James Bond lit a cigarette.
James Bond lit a cigarette.
James Bond lit a cigarette.
James Bond lit a cigarette.

1. A familiar and often repeated action for James Bond that appears verbatim in many 007 novels. All other written text is original commentary based on this action.

James Bond lit a cigarette.

James Bond lit a cigarette.
James Bond lit a cigarette.
James Bond lit a cigarette.
James Bond lit a cigarette.
James Bond lit a cigarette.
James Bond lit a cigarette.
James Bond lit a cigarette.
James Bond lit a cigarette.
James Bond lit a cigarette.

James Bond liked his special blend cigarettes.
James Bond liked his special blend cigarettes.
James Bond liked his special blend cigarettes.
James Bond liked his special blend cigarettes.
James Bond liked his special blend cigarettes.

James Bond disliked Virginia tobacco.

James Bond sat back and lit a cigarette.
James Bond sat back and lit a cigarette.
James Bond sat back and lit a cigarette.
James Bond sat back and lit a cigarette.
James Bond sat back and lit a cigarette.
James Bond sat back and lit a cigarette.
James Bond sat back and lit a cigarette.

James Bond reached for his cigarettes.

James Bond lit another cigarette.
James Bond lit another cigarette.
James Bond lit another cigarette.
James Bond lit another cigarette.
James Bond lit another cigarette.
James Bond lit another cigarette.
James Bond lit another cigarette.
James Bond lit another cigarette.
James Bond lit another cigarette.
James Bond lit another cigarette.
James Bond lit another cigarette.
James Bond lit another cigarette.
James Bond lit another cigarette.
James Bond lit another cigarette.
James Bond lit another cigarette.
James Bond lit another cigarette.
James Bond lit another cigarette.
James Bond lit another cigarette.
James Bond lit another cigarette.
James Bond lit another cigarette.
James Bond lit another cigarette.
James Bond lit another cigarette.
James Bond lit another cigarette.
James Bond lit another cigarette.
James Bond lit another cigarette.

James Bond lit another cigarette.

James Bond lit another cigarette.

James Bond lit another cigarette.

James Bond lit another cigarette.

James Bond lit another cigarette.

James Bond lit another cigarette. `

James Bond lit another cigarette.

James Bond lit another cigarette.

James Bond lit another cigarette.

James Bond finished his drink and lit a cigarette.

James Bond finished his drink and lit a cigarette.

James Bond finished his drink and lit a cigarette.

James Bond finished his cigarette and had another drink.

James Bond finished his cigarette and had another drink.

James Bond finished his cigarette and had another drink.

James Bond finished his cigarette and had another drink.

James Bond finished his cigarette and had another drink. But who was the girl? What was her name? When could he reveal himself to her? (Not now, not now.)

James Bond stabbed out his cigarette, took another out of his gunmetal case, and lit it.

James Bond took in the scene at the casino, ordered another drink, and lit a cigarette.

James Bond sat back and thought for a moment. He lit a cigarette and ordered a drink for himself and the girl.

James Bond sat back and thought for a moment. He reached for a cigarette. He'd had two double bourbons. He ordered another. He would go on ordering another.

James Bond rocked back on his heels and thought for a moment. He paused, and then reached for a cigarette. Would the cigarette someday reach for him? It was a foolish thought. He pushed it from his mind. He thought dismally of sleep.

James Bond was on an island without any cigarettes. His gun was wet and waterlogged, and the girl he'd picked up on the beach collecting shells wasn't turning into a cigarette any time soon. He cursed aloud. —————, he said harshly, because his curses always went unnamed.

James Bond took out his lighter and a cigarette.

James Bond took out his gunmetal case and his lighter and a cigarette, his twentieth of the day.

James Bond lit his seventieth cigarette of the day. The villain would have to wait, but the girls—

James Bond lit his seventieth cigarette of the day. The girl would have to wait, but the villain—

James Bond lit out after the villain; it was his seventieth villain of the day. The girl would have to wait. (Surprise.)

James Bond lit out after the girl; she was his twentieth of the day, and he was failing by about five. The villain wasn't going anywhere underneath that pile of bird shit, so Bond lit a cigarette, inhaled the girl deeply. The cigarette would have to wait, burning like the girl and the villain—Bond cursed them for making him love them and then lit another. *But which one should I light, he had whispered fiercely to himself as he grabbed his lighter. Which one?* (Delight.)

James Bond lit his first delicious cigarette, his first delicious girl. He was delirious and covered in blood; soon he would not know the difference anyway, anyway, he would not know the difference soon.

James Bond wondered if he was about to die, so he reached for a cigarette. He figured things looked pretty bad for him, so he'd buy himself a little time with a smoke while the villain gratified himself with a nice little speech. "For your part," the villain had said before James Bond killed him, "you cannot see further than the gratification of your last cigarette. So enough of this idle chatter."[2] But killing the villain had been pretty gratifying, and James Bond wondered idly if the villain had been right, or if killing every last villain wasn't the immediate gratification Bond couldn't see beyond. Bond staggered a little, realized he was naked, and lit a cigarette. The villain remained dead, and James Bond's cigarette seemed to stay lit longer than usual. (Gratification, indeed.)

James Bond lit his first cigarette with steady, delicious hands.

2. The villain Ernst Stavro Blofeld utters these words before attempting to murder 007 in *You Only Live Twice* (1964).

James Bond concentrated on his hand. The table was hot, and he
was on fire. He lit a cigarette; he had won. (Cards.)
James Bond concentrated. His hands were steady. He lit a cigarette.
It tasted harsh and sweet—deadly, like the girl on the beach. No
wonder she was on fire. (Cliché.)

James Bond lit one with steady hands, drew the smoke and the girl
and the villain and the warm metal gun that had lain against the
skin of his flat stomach into his lungs somehow, all of them, all
at once. Only ten cigarettes remained, and there were two hours
left to go. (Two hours until what?)

James Bond lit into the girl, the villain, his amiable island guide—
everyone within reach; where the hell was his gunmetal case with
his special blend smokes—and the shark repellent?

James Bond lit another cigarette. (Clearly, his gunmetal case and his
special blends had been sent for.) He told the girl who opened the
pack—she reads cards, and she's not really the whore everyone
thinks she is—he told the girl who opened the pack and lit one,
giving it to Bond, "I smoke about three packs a day. You're going
to be busy."[3] And so she would have been, but these girls, they
never live long enough to open another pack. James Bond knows
this is the real crime he would never willingly admit. (Truth.)
James Bond lit another cigarette. His steady hands, his two hours,
and the pack she opened—all these things he drew deeply into

3. James Bond steals the voodoo villain Mr. Big's visionary girl Solitaire and
tells her this as they flee the villain in *Live and Let Die* (1954).

his lungs like the smoke from the smokes he "fluffed" on.

What you do when you're James Bond and you've just lit a cigarette is walk over to the window and stand there, or you throw the pack and the lighter on the counter. Or you throw the villain or the girl on the counter. Or you light another—girl, villain, pack of smokes, depending on how many packs you've smoked so far, and how many girls or villains remain—they'd all be delicious, reassuring, like the sound of the springloaded action of your favorite gun pulled out from underneath your pillow.

James Bond has lit no fewer than ten cigarettes in one day.
James Bond has lit no more than seventy cigarettes in one day. Throw in two bottles of champagne, crushed Benzedrine tablets, and a villain who cheats at cards, and he's got himself a pretty good deal. (Hangover, dry-mouth.)

James Bond helped a pretty girl buy smokes once—the worst kind of smokes so she could quit. "The only way to stop smoking is to stop it and not to start again," James Bond said to the pretty girl. "If you want to *pretend* to stop for a week or two, it's no good trying to ration yourself. You'll become a bore and think about nothing else. And you'll snatch a cigarette every time the hour strikes or whatever the intervals may be. You'll behave greedily. That's unattractive."[4] Is it any wonder she almost died before she had a chance to quit? (Tidy.)

---

4. James Bond steals the missile stealing villa in Emilio Largo's girl Domino, but first he gives her this advice on quitting smoking in *Thunderball* (1961).

James Bond lit a cigarette in Jamaica.

James Bond lit a cigarette in Paris.

James Bond lit a cigarette in Miami.

James Bond lit a cigarette in Vienna.

James Bond lit a cigarette in New York.

James Bond lit a cigarette, and then another, and then another. He was in Turkey. He was in Prague. He was in Vegas. He was not underwater wearing scuba gear, hunting for another man's stolen missiles. He was not ripping the girl he almost loved from a bloodstained sea. Instead, he was hurtling through the dark, soundless night on the Orient Express, and he was about to be killed. (Smoke?)

James Bond lit another cigarette, this time in London where it was raining and he was depressed. The villains had all gone home, and there were no girls on the streets. Peace was killing him. He loved violence. He feared violence. But there was nothing more fearful, depressing, or violent to James Bond than the hollow sound of an empty gunmetal cigarette case, even though he was down to twenty-five cigarettes a day, and failing by about five. (Not unusual. Hardly a surprise.)

James Bond may have smoked in the lavatory.

James Bond lit a cigarette in town, although if you asked him, his selfish car is his only real hobby, and breakfast is his favorite meal of the day.

James Bond lit a cigarette in the country—so much for the nature clinic cure.

James Bond lit a cigarette in his car, at the airport bar, on the golf
course while the rich villain cheated his way through every last
hole. James Bond won anyway, proving that it pays to smoke
while smoking the bastard villain at golf. (Juvenile.)

James Bond lit a cigarette in the casino. He lit another on the way to
his hotel room. He would light another when he sat down on the
bed—he knew he would—especially after he slipped his favorite
gun underneath his pillow. He never told anyone he did this, and
the girls, they never noticed, or they never asked. (Not unusual.
Hardly a surprise.)

James Bond let a man pick him up in a bar once. I know what it
looks like, but it wasn't anything like that. The man had a job
for Bond, and Bond was well on his way to getting drunk after a
dirty job that had left the blood of a defenseless girl on his hands.
So if he was smoking and drinking more than usual—and ac-
cepting employment offers from relative strangers—well, Bond
would let the man offer him whatever he wanted, but Bond drew
the line at letting another man light his cigarette for him. (Not
unusual. Hardly a surprise.)

James Bond's villains—they all belong to him, which he would
know if he weren't so busy lighting up—James Bond's villains
never smoke. They don't really drink either. Don't believe in
it. Isn't that interesting? Banal? Wildly surprising? The world's
worst criminals, the best criminal minds? What does this mean?
Healthy villains make better or stranger targets? But they're usu-
ally also sexless and deformed—no hands, metal eyeballs, heart

on the wrong side of the chest, and their hot girl assistants aren't even really "beards"—faced with such adversity, who would blame villains like these for taking up bad habits like this—smoking? Or would the smokes suppress or curb their grosser appetites—like, say, for world domination? Maybe smokeless villains are just what the world needs, or James Bond would be out of a job. His own appetite for destruction isn't enough to carry the day. (Not unusual. Hardly a surprise.)

What does it mean when James Bond *gradually* draws the smoke into his lungs? When he does this, elegantly, his legs crossed, having just shrugged his shoulders with his gunmetal case, fully stocked, sitting nearby—foolishly, I want to know: Is he in Paris? Jamaica? London? Istanbul? Has his friend been killed yet, the blood from the dying man's veins pooling on the floor of the speeding train while Bond turns away from the grim scene, lights up grimly, and grimly walks off down the long dark hallway? (Grim.)

What does it mean when James Bond swears that he's down to ten cigarettes a day and has not had a single drink? Do you believe him when he says he can swim all day without getting tired? Who swims all day on ten cigarettes without tiring, without even a single drink? Offer him a smoke, see if he takes it, a whisky, too, and watch him sit back and shrug off his newfound resolve. (Up in smoke.) Watch Bond set grimly to work on the smoking gunmetal girl, sweeping her with the force of ten thousand *gradually*s softly down into his lungs.

BODY [BOND, JAMES]

(The action: *body*, 1953–1965, 1966)

a.

b.
Bond bowed and drank more sake

c.
Bond choked back the sickness that rose from his stomach into the
    back of his throat
Bond clenched his jaws and half closed his eyes
Bond clenched his teeth
Bond climbed under the single cotton sheet
Bond controlled his rising gorge
Bond crashed headlong into the wine-red floor
Bond cursed himself
Bond cursed softly to himself

d.
Bond decided to give up
Bond dozed wakefully

62

Bond dragged the smoke deep into his lungs
Bond dropped to one knee

e.

f.
Bond felt a lump in his throat
Bond felt a pang of jealousy
Bond felt a surge in terror that almost made him vomit
Bond felt himself starting to vomit
Bond felt his body getting out of control
Bond felt like hell and he knew he also looked it
Bond flicked the lighter
Bond fitted the Beretta into its holster
Bond frowned
Bond frowned

g.
Bond gasped for air
Bond gathered his breath
Bond gave a deep and relaxed sigh
Bond gazed into the beautiful worried eyes
Bond glanced at his watch
Bond glanced at his watch
Bond glimpsed endless miles of palm-lined avenues
Bond got clumsily to his feet, shaking his head
Bond got out of bed and gave himself a cold shower

Bond grimaced and clenched his senses
Bond grinned
Bond grinned apologetically
Bond grinned to himself
Bond gritted his teeth
Bond gritted his teeth and his muscles lumped under his coat
Bond groaned
Bond groaned and lifted his head
Bond ground his teeth
Bond ground his teeth
Bond ground his teeth and shut his mind
Bond grunted noncommittally

Bond gulped down the cool night air

h.
Bond had walked for only a few minutes
Bond hammered with his only free hand
Bond heaved a deep sigh
Bond held his breath

i.

j.
Bond jumped to his feet

k.
Bond knelt on the backseat

l.

Bond laughed

Bond laughed

Bond lay and panted through clenched teeth

Bond lay down on his bed and stared at the ceiling

Bond let out a deep sigh and picked up his discarded cigarette

Bond looked at his fingernails

Bond looked at his watch

Bond looked away from the sprawling figure

Bond looked up into the spangled sky

m.

Bond made a frantic effort to move

Bond made no comment

n.

p.

Bond picked up his cards and his eyes glittered

Bond pitched forward on the floor

Bond put an arm around her and held her to him

Bond put down the receiver

q.

r.

Bond racked his brain for a solution

Bond raised his eyes to hers

Bond raised his head
Bond rubbed his naked shoulder against her

s.
Bond sat for a moment, frozen in his chair
Bond sat on his bed
Bond sauntered on in search of an air-conditioned bar

Bond screwed up his eyes and opened them again
Bond scrubbed the rouge off his lips

Bond shivered
Bond shook himself
Bond shook his head, waiting for the story
Bond shouted
Bond sighed and sat down

Bond shrugged
Bond shrugged
Bond shrugged

Bond shrugged his right shoulder and saved his breath

Bond shrugged his shoulders
Bond shrugged his shoulders
Bond shrugged his shoulders
Bond shrugged his shoulders
Bond shrugged his shoulders

Bond shrugged his shoulders
Bond shrugged his shoulders
Bond shrugged his shoulders
Bond shrugged his shoulders
Bond shrugged his shoulders
Bond shrugged his shoulders
Bond shrugged his shoulders

Bond shrugged his shoulders and moved to the window
Bond shrugged his shoulders and then went back into their sitting
    room
Bond shrugged his shoulders and waited for the steward
Bond shrugged his shoulders and walked quickly to the telephone
Bond shrugged his shoulders impatiently
Bond shrugged his shoulders to lighten his thoughts

Bond shrugged impatiently
Bond shrugged with indifference he didn't feel

Bond shivered
Bond shivered
Bond shivered
Bond shivered slightly
Bond shuddered
Bond shuddered and went on his way
Bond sighed and shrugged his shoulders
Bond slammed the door

Bond smiled
Bond smiled
Bond smiled a thin smile

Bond smiled and grinned slightly
Bond smiled at her and shrugged his shoulders
Bond smiled at the appeal for help
Bond smiled bitterly
Bond smiled cheerfully
Bond smiled down at her
Bond smiled encouragingly
Bond smiled for the first time

Bond smiled grimly
Bond smiled grimly

Bond smiled grimly to himself
Bond smiled grimly to himself

Bond smiled into her grey eyes
Bond smiled ironically at the introspective scrutiny

Bond smiled politely
Bond smiled politely
Bond smiled to himself
Bond smiled stiffly
Bond smiled sympathetically
Bond smiled thinly

Bond smiled thinly
Bond smiled warmly at her
Bond smiled weakly
Bond smiled wryly at his reflection

Bond snorted

Bond squared his shoulders

Bond staggered over to her bed
Bond staggered to his feet, keeping low

Bond stiffened
Bond stirred and felt the prick of a dagger over his kidneys
Bond stood and dripped sweat and blood
Bond stood for a moment gaining his breath
Bond stopped in his tracks
Bond stopped in his tracks
Bond strained his eyes
Bond stretched out with his head in her lap
Bond strolled off in the direction of his bedroom
Bond stumbled over a mangrove root
Bond suddenly felt that he did not know quite enough of the
    answers
Bond suddenly felt that he had had enough of the ghastly glitter

Bond swallowed
Bond swiveled

t.

Bond tensed

Bond tightened his arm around her shoulders

Bond twisted like a dying animal on the ground

Bond twisted to protect his stomach

Bond turned his back on the scene

Bond turned his back on the table

u.

Bond uttered a realistic groan

Bond uttered an animal groan and fainted

v.

Bond verified that his room had been searched

w.

Bond walked over to the bed

Bond was delirious

Bond watched listlessly

Bond waved a cheerful hand

Bond whistled softly

Bond whistled softly and smiled

Bond wiped the cold sweat off his face

Bond wiped the sweat out of his eyes and stood listening

x.

y.

z.

DRINKS [BOND, JAMES]

(The action: *drinks*, 1953–1965, 1966)

Bond*Bond* drinks*drinks* martinis almost exclusively. Bond*Bond* drinks*drinks* Bourbon almost exclusively. Bond*Bond* drinks*drinks* whiskey almost exclusively. Bond*Bond* drinks*drinks* brandy and ginger ale only occasionally. Bond*Bond* drinks*drinks* vintage champagne, usually more than one bottle, and sometimes alone, sometimes with a girl, and sometimes with his boss. Bond*Bond* drinks*drinks* vodka with black pepper to sink impurities like fusel oil to the bottom of the glass. Bond*Bond* drinks*drinks* schnapps in a flask on the go. Bond*Bond* drinks*drinks* coffee with brandy. Bond*Bond* drinks*drinks* vodka tonics with a slice of lemon peel.

Only rarely does Bond*Bond* drink*drink* scotch and sodas. Bond*Bond* takes heavy slugs, stiff pulls, and long deep swallows. Bond*Bond* sips. Bond*Bond* orders, pours, watches drunkenly. Bond's*Bond's* drinks*drinks* are doubled and doubled again, served on the rocks or with soda or branch water or bitters. There are deep champagne glasses and balloon glasses. There are bottles, half bottles, and half glasses. There are pints. There are no last calls. There are hangovers, but only rarely. There are amphetamines, especially with champagne and cards. Glasses materialize with a half bottle on the green baize where Bond*Bond* has just relieved the villain of his money at cards.

Sometimes there is gin. Sometimes there is coffee, black and strong and to the brim, or Turkish and thick with grains. Sometimes there are unnamed drinks*drinks*, which Bond*Bond* finishes sullenly, handsomely, grimly, by the glass and the bottle and the pint and the flask, because they are dry, doubled, and pooling before his cruel mouth. Bond*Bond* orders vaguely and with feelings of treachery creeping in-between him and the girl. Bond*Bond* drinks*drinks* guiltily, after a cold shower, and just before bed where sleep is most often immediate and sound. Bond's*Bond's* drinks*drinks* double when his stakes do. Bond's*Bond's* vodkas double when the girls do. Bond's*Bond's* girls double when the scotch and sodas do. Bond's*Bond's* guilt doubles when the numbers of dead girls do, so keep the doubles coming. Bond's*Bond's* unnamed curses, drinks*drinks*, and girls double when the villain's stolen missiles do. Bond's*Bond's* conscience doubled is a little like half a glass of villain with a lemon peel, a bottle of girl, and a couple of heavy slugs of treachery on the rocks. Bond's*Bond's* villain doubled is like a bottle of bottles, glasses of glass, and heavy slugs of drunkenly on the rocks.

Sometimes when Bond's*Bond's* conscience is doubled, there is grimly, black pepper, and numbers, so keep the curses coming. Sometimes when Bond's*Bond's* double is doubled, there is beer. There is flask. There is sullenly. There is heavy. There is money, unnamed, mouth. Grain when the glass rocks. Handsome oil sound occasional fusel bitters. Girls. Dead sip doubled. Swallowed peel another cold. Grimly just before dry. Served exclusively, very cold. Brim.

GUN [BOND, JAMES]

(The action: *gun*, 1953–1965, 1966)

_____ _____ likes his _____
warm, underneath his pillow, and sometimes cold against the skin
of his flat stomach where it's almost always tucked firmly into his
waistband. The _____ may be wet or waterlogged,
or _____ _____ may carry it between his
teeth—whatever it takes for _____ _____
to remain armed. The make and model may change, but the results
are pretty much the same: _____ _____'s
_____ signs death sentences. _____
_____'s _____ effects introductions.
_____ _____'s _____ is con-
cealed among the rags of his clothing on the desert island where
_____ _____ hunts the villain with sin-
gle-minded resolve. But sometimes the caliber changes. Some-
times the make and model change. Sometimes _____
_____'s _____ winds up in the wrong
hands, the hands of the opposition—and doesn't _____
_____ feel stupid when the man he's mistaken
for a brother in arms turns out to be his executioner. Unless

_____ _____ can turn things around pretty quick, _____ _____ is staring down the barrel of his own _____, which is pretty embarrassing. ("Bit on the light side," _____ _____ had said when he handed his _____ over, "but it'll kill if you put the bullets in the right places."[1]) Some of _____ _____'s finest moments are with his _____— _____ _____ meditates on his long "marriage" to it; _____ _____ dismantles and dries it on the beach while his shell-collecting honey wonders at the sight of it—this is also when _____ _____ finds he's reassured by the _____'s healthy reassembled sound; _____ _____ holsters it; _____ _____ feels "naked" without it; _____ _____ hates it when someone, anyone touches it; _____ _____ can't fall asleep without it—always the right hand moves to the butt of the _____ underneath his pillow while sleep overtakes him; _____ _____ likes the heavy metal feeling against his skin, whatever the caliber, make or model; _____ _____ smiles grimly at the thought of it; _____ _____ waves the enemy forward with it. _____ _____'s opened wide for it himself, carrying his _____ in his mouth while he crawled on hands and knees toward freedom and release. _____ _____'s practiced shooting himself in the wardrobe

---

1. Bond utters these words in *From Russia With Love* (1957) just before putting his gun in the hands of a Russian executioner he thought was a brother in arms.

mirror (one wonders: are objects larger than they appear), has pumped rounds into beds in hotel rooms around the world before disappearing into the night to face whatever villain awaits him. It's usually better for _____ _____ if the odds are against him; the villain's got to have far more firepower than _____ _____ 's own little _____ is capable of producing. But the trouble with the villain's firepower is easily discovered—and _____ _____ usually does, usually—the trouble with the villain's firepower is that it's usually not his own. It's stolen, secretly amassed, which means it's not legit—ineffective; it's always returned to its rightful, peace-loving owners who don't know how it could have fallen into the wrong hands. This is when _____ _____ restores order and world peace, even when his _____ has gone missing, which is the real puzzler, practically and psychoanalytically speaking. For the matter of that, _____ _____'s _____ jammed on him once. _____ _____'s boss got wind of it and made _____ _____ get a new one, which is pretty embarrassing when you're _____ _____ and suddenly your boss is thinking the _____ you've always trusted has absolutely no stopping power. But there is good news for _____ _____ and his new _____. _____ _____ can get ammunition for it anywhere in the world, and it's much quicker on the draw. But this issue of legitimacy is an interesting one, given comparative size and power—also girls, who rarely get to hold a _____, not even when they're working in the service of the fleshy asexual

villain who wants his gold, diamonds, cash whatever the cost and
by whatever means necessary—*okay, okay*, I get it: with or without
his smoking-wet-reassembled _____, _____
_____ and his _____ are *legit*. But to sur-
vive, to carry the day in any convincing way, _____
_____ needs a villain, plenty of mirrors, a hard butt,
and a dumb girl who wouldn't know what to do with a piece of fire-
power unless _____ _____ decided he'd take
the time to teach her, which _____ _____
almost always, almost never does.

HEART [BOND, JAMES]

(The action: *heart*, 1953—1965, 1966)

1. Bond's heart _____ at the sight of her.
    a. *hammered* b. *lifted* c. *sang* d. *warmed* e. *went cold*
2. Bond's heart _____ at the thought of sporting with the villain at golf.
    a. *hammered* b. *lifted* c. *sang* d. *warmed* e. *went cold*
3. Bond's heart _____ and he cursed himself and the girl under his breath for their carelessness.
    a. *hammered* b. *lifted* c. *sang* d. *warmed* e. *went cold*
4. Bond's heart _____ when the villain's eyes seemed to bore into Bond's brain.
    a. *hammered* b. *lifted* c. *sang* d. *warmed* e. *went cold*
5. Bond's heart _____ at the villain's misstep, and Bond smiled softly to himself.
    a. *hammered* b. *lifted* c. *sang* d. *warmed* e. *went cold*
6. Bond knew his men were ready to fight until the last harpoon had been fired, but which of them would reach the surface

again? Bond's heart _____ and he swam on.

a. *hammered* b. *lifted* c. *sang* d. *warmed* e. *went cold*

7. Bond's heart _____ at the thought of killing the villain in his island hideout with a waterlogged gun, but he resolved to try before it rusted and the villain fled.

   a. *hammered* b. *lifted* c. *sang* d. *warmed* e. *went cold*

8. Bond's heart _____ at the prospect of reversing his recent bad fortune with a tough job.

   a. *hammered* b. *lifted* c. *sang* d. *warmed* e. *went cold*

9. (Bond thought idly of her prudish beauty, which would also be a shame to lose if the girl was now dead.) Bond's heart _____ at the prospect of being blown to bits.

   a. *hammered* b. *lifted* c. *sang* d. *warmed* e. *went cold*

10. Bond's heart _____ at the knowledge this could be their last moment together. So much for love.

    a. *hammered* b. *lifted* c. *sang* d. *warmed* e. *went cold*

11. Bond's heart _____ as the roulette wheel whirred. He was dangerously close to losing it all.

    a. *hammered* b. *lifted* c. *sang* d. *warmed* e. *went cold*

BLOOD [BOND, JAMES]

(The action: *blood*, 1953—1965, 1966)[1]

_____ 1. bleeding (*bond / girl / villain / other*)
_____ 2. blood (*bond / girl / villain / other*)
_____ 3. blood-flecked (*bond / girl / villain / other*)
_____ 4. bloodied (*bond / girl / villain / other*)
_____ 5. blood-letting (*bond / girl / villain / other*)
_____ 6. bloodlust (*bond / girl / villain / other*)
_____ 7. blood pressure (*bond / girl / villain / other*)
_____ 8. blood-red (*bond / girl / villain / other*)
_____ 9. bloodshot (*bond / girl / villain / other*)
_____ 10. blood-soaked (*bond / girl / villain / other*)
_____ 12. blood-stained (*bond / girl / villain / other*)
_____ 13. blood stream (*bond / girl / villain / other*)
_____ 14. blood-warm (*bond / girl / villain / other*)
_____ 15. bloody (*bond / girl / villain / other*)
_____ 16. full-blooded (*bond / girl / villain / other*)

1. Bond novels are pretty bloodless, but these are the bloody options most often named in 007's world.

COLD [BOND, JAMES]

(The action: *cold*, 1953—1965, 1966)

1. suicide note	a. cold
2. world domination	b. coolly
3. thrilling passion	c. coldness
4. sparkling eyes	d. coldly
5. roulette table	e. coolness
6. foul golf balls	f. cold-hearted
7. arrogant body	g. cold, hard—
8. cruel smile	h. ice-cold
9. waterlogged gun	i. cold-heartedly
10. sputtering breath	j. cool, deliciously—
11. bottomless chair	k. cool and quizzical—
12. thundering avalanche	l. chilled
13. selfish car	m. chill in the—
14. stolen kimono	n. beautifully cool—
15. double agent girlfriend	o. cold breath of—
16. wedded bliss	p. frigid

PAIN [BOND, JAMES]

(The action: *pain*, 1953—1965, 1966)

arduous climb, battered body shattering the sea, bloodletting, bloodshot eyes, blood blooming, bloody bait, a bloody beautiful girl, bloody muscles screaming, bloody wedded bliss, bloody voodoo, blistered flesh, blown to bits, burning ribs, dangerous fumes, exploding cliffs, funereal flowers, a giant blow, lengthy seductions, love in Turkey, love on holiday, a tender delirium, a tender kiss in captivity, suffocation by gold paint, suicide, stolen soul, swollen wrists, the shock of bullets, shots fired from a golden gun, shower of bloody flesh simple ardor

KISS [BOND, JAMES]

(The action: *kiss*, 1953—1965, 1966)

___ 1. James Bond kissed her tenderly . . .

___ 2. James Bond kissed her passionately . . .

___ 3. James Bond kissed her cruelly . . .

___ 4. James Bond kissed her eyes . . .

___ 5. James Bond kissed her cheeks . . .

___ 6. James Bond kissed her hard on the mouth . . .

___ 7. James Bond kissed her once . . .

___ 8. James Bond kissed her fiercely and cruelly . . .

___ 9. James Bond kissed her softly on half-open lips . . .

___ 10. James Bond kissed her in the velvety tropical air of night . . .

___ 11. James Bond kissed her good-night . . .

___ 12. James Bond kissed her once more and stepped away . . .

___ 13. James Bond kissed her in the villain's underground lair . . .

___ 14. James Bond kissed her occasionally . . .

___ 15. James Bond admitted the kiss was a splendid one . . .

1 = every day   2 = occasionally   3 = always   4 = never

TIRED [BOND, JAMES]

(The action: *tired*, 1953—1965, 1966)

_____ 1. James Bond was tired of being tough, though he would never say so.

_____ 2. James Bond was tired. In truth, these damn villains exhausted him.

_____ 3. James Bond slept a shallow, nervous sleep. Was he in love?

_____ 4. James Bond was delirious with lack of sleep, which unnerved him.

_____ 5. James Bond stumbled. He was weak with nervous exhaustion.

_____ 6. James Bond wondered if he looked as tired and stale as he felt.

_____ 7. James Bond was immediately asleep with his hand on his gun.

_____ 8. James Bond dozed with a book on his chest. The villains could wait.

_____ 9. James Bond fell wearily onto the bed alone, for which he was glad.

_____ 10. James Bond slept on board the train and wondered about the girl.

_____ 11. James Bond slept in the plane and dreamed about the girl.

_____ 12. James Bond was drowsy, and he knew he would be tired for days.

_____ 13. James Bond looked like death he was so weary. What a nightmare.

_____ 14. James Bond dozed with his gun in his hand, waiting for the villain.

_____ 15. James Bond's mind had shut down, too tired to cope or to care.

1 = totally acceptable 2 = partially acceptable 3 = unacceptable
4 = don't know

[A U T O] B I O G R A P H Y

Sylvia   Trench   sits   across   the   game   table
from   James   Bond   at a London   hotel   in   the
1962   film *Dr. No*   She's losing   big   and   she's
borrowing   more money   against   the   house   *The*
house   will   cover the   difference   she   insists   She
doesn't   ask   She   could be   a   little   more   concerned
Bond   has   the   shoe   and   the winning   hand   He   looks
up   from   his   hand   and   says   *I admire   your   courage*
Ms   His   voice   trails   off   and he feigns   a   casual
disinterested   air   Maybe   he   really   is disinterested   But
that's   ridiculous   What   does   Trench   think   she's doing
here   Bond   reaches   for   his   cigarette   case   Trench
reaches   for   her   pocketbook   How   much   is   she
willing to   put   down   Her   eyebrow   goes   up   *Trench*
Sylvia Trench   I   admire   your   luck   Mr   she pauses he says
Bond James Bond   The   Bond   theme   song   begins   to
play   before   he   can   say *Bond*   a   second   time   *Mr*
Bond   Ms. Trench   says   eyebrow   raised   cool   and
oozing   seduction   *I   suppose   you   wouldn't   care   to*
raise the   limits   She   is   the   perfect   picture   of   Sixties
chic   in   a   red   chiffon   dress   with   her   red   lips and

her heavily-lined eyelids Sitting down at the game table she is all eyes and shoulders and sweeping hair and she sparkles like that jewel of a brooch she's wearing *I have no objections* Bond says with an imperceptible smile and a wave of his hand cigarette held idly between his fingers Sylvia thinks she can turn the tables on him She's an idle threat and the deck seems stacked against her Bond deals the cards looks at Trench and says *Looks like you're out to get me* I've watched the opening scene with Trench and Bond several times now She's the only girl at the table What are the stakes Bond's winning and she's losing and that's not likely to change It's nice that she tries Should someone tell her Would she listen It's not until he's called away from the table that I realize Trench wants in on the game no matter the odds and no matter the cost By the time he's asked her if she *plays any other games I mean besides Chemine de fer* I'm captivated by how carnal appetites are conveyed wave of a wrist heady eye contact sweet swirl of cigarette smoke placing and raising of bets Trench seems to know what she's up against Who writes this stuff and avoids the innuendo She thinks she's in on the game Bond seems to know better He wins wins again and tosses his last hand on the table She thought things would turn out differently Even as Bond has the upper

hand   in   boudoirs around   the   world   even   if   the
world   still   belonged   to   men   like   Bond   so   much
the   better   for   girls   like Trench   who   make   a   smoky
gaming   table   a   thrilling   scene   of   seduction   for
girls   willing   to wager

As   it   turns   out   she's   always   got   golf   to   fall back
on   if   teeing   off   in   Bond's   bedroom   counts   for
anything   and   I'm   not   sure   it   doesn't   What kind   of
currency   does   Trench   have   beyond   the   sex with   Bond
we   don't   actually   see   or   does   she   trade   in   or   on
saucy   red   dresses   for   respectability   she   won't ever   have
like   Bond   Girls   do   Does   her   sexual   currency preclude
everything   but   seduction   I'm   watching the scene   where
Trench   stands   alluring   as   hell   with Bond   in   the
Casino's foyer   and   Bond   stands   beside   her charmed
and   charming   And   here's   Trench   raising   that right
eyebrow   so   high   it's   almost   ridiculous   *Too   bad
you have   to   go*   she's   just   murmured   *just   as   things
were getting   interesting*   I   wonder   why   Bond   isn't   more
taken in   by   her   lips   and   fluttering   lids   She's   carried
that eyebrow   and   her   gold   handbag   across   the   casino
floor like   prize-winning   chips   I'd   say   the   brow's   the
better   accessory   but   don't   overdo   it Sylvia   It's   some
fantastic   high   brow   flirting   and   doesn't   the   very idea
of   Bond   lend   itself   to   fabulous excess   Bond's   cashed
in   his   chips   Sylvia's   cashed   in   on   Bond   Should she
take   a   certain   satisfaction   in   her   dress   jewels   and

her well-heeled   gold   shoes   Is   Trench   well-heeled having
gotten   Bond's   attention too

Trench   is   so   savvy   she   could   seduce   the pants
off   the   unerring   007   just   as   fast   as   he   could
mount   an   offensive   against   her   And she does   While
Bond   is   at   MI6   getting   his   next   assignment
Trench has   let   herself   into Bond's   apartment   where
she   has   changed   into   one   of   his   dress   shirts   She
keeps her   gold   heels   on   Her   thick   brown   hair   hangs
loose   in   curls   around   her   face   and   her   lips   shine
a   glossy   red She   is   the   site   of   a   complex   and
contradictory   sexuality   by   advancing   on   Bond   by
putting   in his bedroom   when   he   walks   in   the   front
door   In   a   minute he'll   be   on   his   knees   in   the
doorway   gun   aimed   from the   camera's   vantage   point
at   the   space   between   Sylvia's   legs   Is   it   possible
that   she   is seduction because   she   wishes   it   and   not
simply   because Bond appreciates   a   worthy   adversary
Thinking   he's   about to be ambushed   he   shuts   off   the
lights   He's   not   wrong   but   it's   not   what   he
expected   He   swings   open the   door   to   his   bedroom
and   there   with   her buttocks barely   exposed   stands
Sylvia   murmuring   something about having   accepted
Bond's invitation   She's   playing   her game in the   boudoir
with   Bond's   own   balls   though   it is possible she   brought
her own   Whatever the case   she's got   Bond by the golf balls
She's   sure   Bond   won't   mind

There she says a talking pair of legs because that's all we see as her legs fill the screen *Now you made me miss it* The way the shot is framed Trench's legs rival the doorway for sheer height and her club dwarfs Bond's gun But that won't matter A club's not a gun and not in the wrong hands *You don't miss a thing* Bond says and closes the door *How did you get in here* And before she can answer *Never mind that now you're here* He's not surprised but he could be just a bit more delighted Even Bond has his limits or is it just a matter of time He's about to tell her he's got to leave *immediately* or *almost immediately* and still putting and pouting in his bedroom is Sylvia When a woman needs saving the world can wait Or how about this one a woman's got to know how to lose and she's got to know when to get lost And silly seductive Sylvia's gotten them mixed up again *I decided to accept your invitation* she says as she busies herself with his golf balls He reaches to conceal his weapon *That was for tomorrow afternoon* he says hardly bothered She leans in slides her arms around his neck He's checking his watch He's checking out her follow-through They kiss and the scene ends as quickly as it began He leaves for his mission and we never see Trench again But she's made an impression because we assume she got what she came for

But it's Honey   Rider, I remember   in   the   film who
walks   out of the ocean   and   onto   the   beach   at   Crab
Key   wearing   a   bikini with   a   knife   attached   while
Bond   sleeps   in   a   mangrove close   to   shore   curled   up
in   the   sand   with   his gun   Honey looks   like   Venus
in   the   flesh   rising   from   the   waves   She's holding
some   shells   and   singing   an island   tune   when Bond
joins   in   having   been   awakened   by   her   song   His
gun has got   to see   this   Bond   is   on   his   feet   leaning
with his   left   hand   against   a   palm   tree   wide-eyed
like I've never   seen   him   because   Honey's   like   nothing
he's ever seen   She   stands   tan   and   long-limbed   under
an   overcast   sky the perfect   green   sea   behind her   Even
her   lashes   are   long   With   big   seashells   and   her
perfect   white bikini Honey's   no   ordinary   trespasser
She's   sailed   on   her own from mainland   Jamaica   to this
hidden   island   in pursuit of seashells   she   can   sell for
cash   And   she   might have made it home   with   her   stolen
booty   had   she not   met   Bond on the beach hidden
there   in the   mangrove   telling   Honey   he's   not supposed
to be there He   takes   it   she isn't   either

Have   they   both come   to   the island   looking for   trouble
Honey   for   her   seashells   and   Bond for his villain
They're both wandering   about   where   they   don't belong
What   good   can   come of it   As   it   happens Honey's
unknowingly   alerted   the villain to Bond's   presence   on
the   island   and   soon   she'll   be   caught   in the

crossfire laying low in the mangroves with Bond
and his waterlogged gun while the villain's goons
try flushing them out with gunfire Her skiff will
be shot through with holes and Bond's plan for
flushing out evil will be shot through with Honey She'll be
stranded He'll think he's saddled with a half-naked goddess
in the flesh and how's he going to catch the villain
while trailing a girl That's moments from now and
Honey and Bond still have to get to know each
other She squints into the sun *What are you doing
here Looking for shells* Honey's taken a step back
though I've already gotten the impression she won't lose
any ground Her brow is furrowed ever so slightly I
wouldn't cross her She's got her knife in her hand
now all her shells in the other She's come this far and
Bond has come far enough *Stay where you are* she tells
him Twice Bond's promised he won't touch her seashells
Honey's promised him he won't either The last man
who went for her "shells" wound up dead Spider
bite Black widow Honey's not one to mess around
She is fearless and afraid the perfect combination
of toughness and vulnerability Who does she think
she is but sex and death devourer and devoured I am
watching James Bond and Honey Rider and at this
moment I wonder who I would rather be